Messages of Faith

Colorful Blessings

Messages of Faith

A COLORING BOOK OF FAITHFUL EXPRESSION

ILLUSTRATIONS BY DEBORAH MULLER

ST. MARTIN'S GRIFFIN

NEW YORK

COLORFUL BLESSINGS: MESSAGES OF FAITH.

Copyright © 2017 by St. Martin's Press. All rights reserved. Printed in the United States of America. For information, address St. Martin's Press, 175 Fifth Avenue, New York, N.Y. 10010.

www.stmartins.com

All scripture quotations are taken from:

The Holy Bible, King James Version. Cambridge Edition: 1769; King James Bible Online, 2017

ISBN 978-1-250-14165-1 (trade paperback)

Our books may be purchased in bulk for promotional, educational, or business use.

Please contact your local bookseller or the Macmillan Corporate and Premium

Sales Department at 1-800-221-7945, extension 5442, or by e-mail

at MacmillanSpecialMarkets@macmillan.com.

First Edition: October 2017

10 9 8 7 6 5 4 3 2 1

Let love be without dissimulation. Abhor that which is evil;

cleave to that which is good

Romans 12:9

But without faith it is impossible to please him: for he that cometh to God must believe that he is, and that he is a rewarder of them that diligently seek him.

Hebrews 11:6

He healeth the broken in heart

psalm 147:3

And all things, whatsoever ye shall ask
in prayer, believing, ye shall receive.

Matthew 21:22

And Jesus answering saith unto them,
Have faith in God.

Mark 11:22

He's after your heart

Deuteronomy 30:16

For by grace are ye saved through faith; and that not of yourselves: it is the gift of God.

Ephesians 2:8

Let brotherly love Continue

Hebrews 13:1

For I have said, Mercy shall be built
up for ever: thy faithfulness shalt thou
establish in the very heavens.

Psalm 89:2

WE LOVE HIM because HE first loved US

1 John 4:19

O love the Lord, all ye his saints: for the Lord preserveth the faithful, and plentifully rewardeth the proud doer.

Psalm 31:23

Because thy loving kindness is better than life

Psalm 63:3

He that is faithful in that which
is least is faithful also in much:
and he that is unjust in the least
is unjust also in much.

Luke 16:10

PUT OTHERS FIRST

Be kindly affectioned one to another with brotherly love; in honour preferring one another; Romans 12:10

For with God nothing shall
be impossible.

Luke 1:37

John 3:16

Now faith is the substance of things hoped for, the evidence of things not seen.

Hebrews 11:1

First, I thank my God through
Jesus Christ for you all,
that your faith is spoken of
throughout the whole world.

Romans 1:8

Trust in the LORD with all
thine heart; and lean not unto
thine own understanding.

Proverbs 3:5

Be Wise and guide thine heart in the way

Proverbs 23:19

O Lord God of hosts, who is a
strong Lord like unto thee? or to thy
faithfulness round about thee?

Psalm 89:8

That your faith should not stand
in the wisdom of men, but in the
power of God.

1 Corinthians 2:5

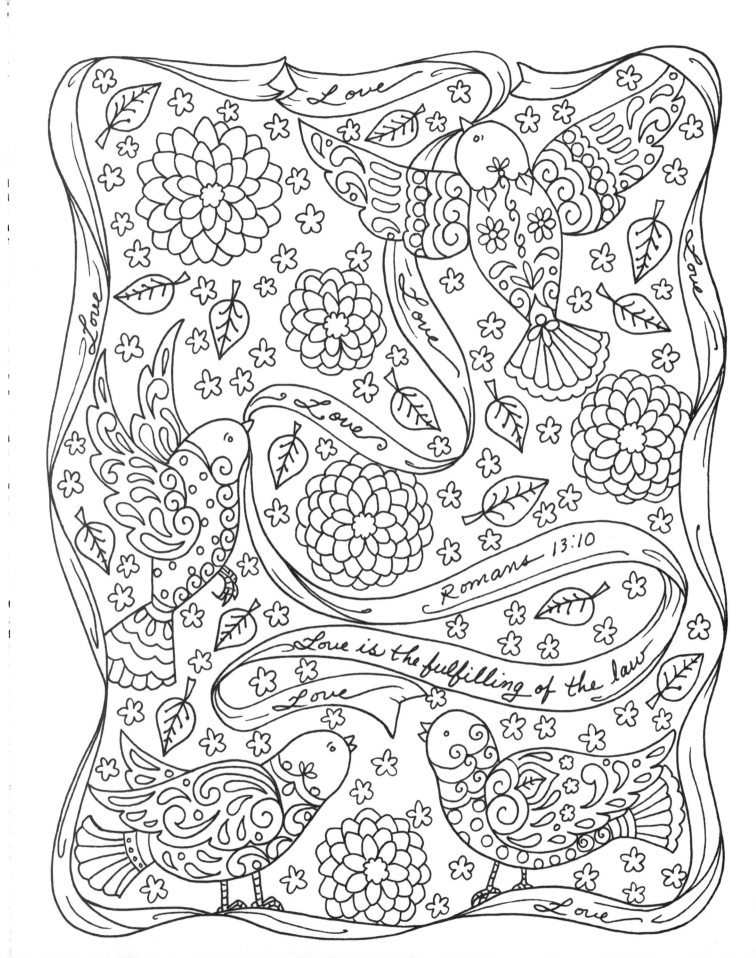

Thy testimonies that thou hast
commanded are righteous and
very faithful.

Psalm 119:138

A merry heart maketh a cheerful countenance

Proverbs 15:13

Ye see then how that by
works a man is justified,
and not by faith only.

James 2:24

What doth it profit, my brethren, though
a man say he hath faith, and have not
works? can faith save him?

James 2:14

For we walk by faith, not by sight.

2 Corinthians 5:7

He staggered not at the promise of God through unbelief; but was strong in faith, giving glory to God;

Romans 4:20

For therein is the righteousness of
God revealed from faith to faith: as it
is written, The just shall live by faith.

Romans 1:17

Who are kept by the power of God through faith unto salvation ready to be revealed in the last time.

1 Peter 1:5

PSALM 127:2

Wherefore also we pray always for you,
that our God would count you worthy
of this calling, and fulfil all the good
pleasure of his goodness, and the work
of faith with power:

2 Thessalonians 1:11

Even the righteousness of God which
is by faith of Jesus Christ unto all and
upon all them that believe: for there
is no difference:

Romans 3:22

I am crucified with Christ:
nevertheless I live; yet not I, but
Christ liveth in me: and the life which
I now live in the flesh I live by the
faith of the Son of God, who loved me,
and gave himself for me.

Galatians 2:20

But that no man is justified by the
law in the sight of God, it is evident:
for, The just shall live by faith.

Galatians 3:11

For I say, through the grace given unto
me, to every man that is among you,
not to think of himself more highly
than he ought to think; but to think
soberly, according as God hath dealt to
every man the measure of faith.

Romans 12:3

For ye are all the children of God
by faith in Christ Jesus.

Galatians 3:26

Looking unto Jesus the author and
finisher of our faith; who for the joy that
was set before him endured the cross,
despising the shame, and is set down at
the right hand of the throne of God.

Hebrews 12:2

Beloved, let us love one another: for love is of God; and every one that loveth is born of God, and knoweth God.

1 John 4:7

To shew forth thy loving kindness
in the morning, and thy faithfulness
every night.

Psalm 92:2

Many waters cannot quench love, neither can the floods drown it: if a man would give all the substance of his house for love, it would utterly be contemned. Song of Solomon 8:7

For whatsoever is born of God overcometh the world: and this is the victory that overcometh the world, even our faith.

1 John 5:4

I will sing of the mercies of the
Lord forever: with my mouth will
I make known thy faithfulness to
all generations.

Psalm 89:1

Love beareth all things

1 Corintians 13:7

But my faithfulness and my mercy
shall be with him: and in my name
shall his horn be exalted.

Psalm 89:24

Thy mercy, O Lord, is in the heavens;
and thy faithfulness reacheth unto
the clouds.

Psalm 36:5

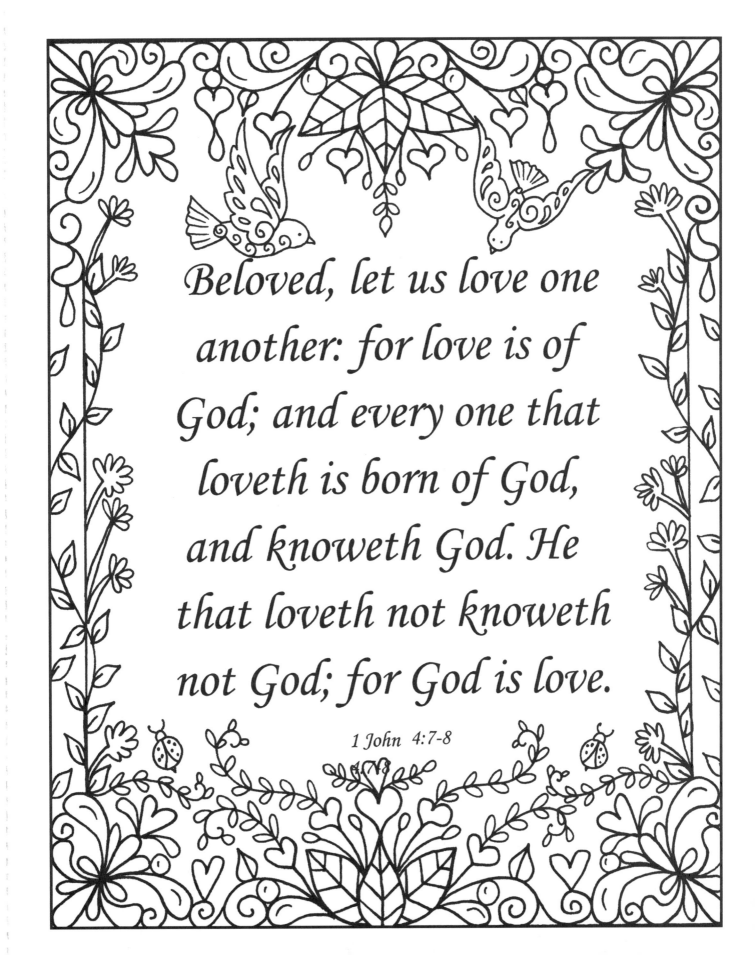

Beloved, let us love one another: for love is of God; and every one that loveth is born of God, and knoweth God. He that loveth not knoweth not God; for God is love.

1 John 4:7-8

But Jesus turned him about, and when he saw her, he said, Daughter, be of good comfort; thy faith hath made thee whole. And the woman was made whole from that hour.

Matthew 9:22

By whom also we have access by faith
into this grace wherein we stand, and
rejoice in hope of the glory of God.

Romans 5:2

Therefore leaving the principles of
the doctrine of Christ, let us go on
unto perfection; not laying again the
foundation of repentance from dead
works, and of faith toward God.

Hebrews 6:1

Act in such a matter that you are living proof of a loving God.

They are new every morning:
great is thy faithfulness.

Lamentations 3:23

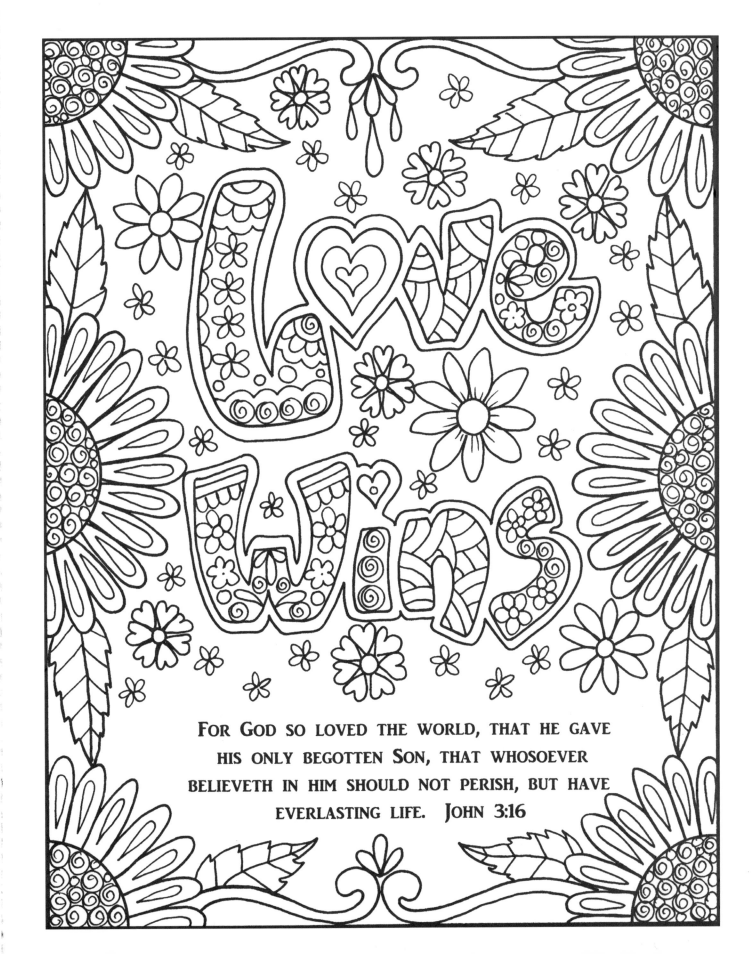

Love Wins

FOR GOD SO LOVED THE WORLD, THAT HE GAVE HIS ONLY BEGOTTEN SON, THAT WHOSOEVER BELIEVETH IN HIM SHOULD NOT PERISH, BUT HAVE EVERLASTING LIFE. JOHN 3:16

So that we ourselves glory in you in
the churches of God for your patience
and faith in all your persecutions and
tribulations that ye endure:

2 Thessalonians 1:4

But God commendeth his love toward us, in that, while we were yet sinners, Christ died for us.

Romans 5:8

Whom God hath set forth to be a
propitiation through faith in his
blood, to declare his righteousness
for the remission of sins that are past,
through the forbearance of God;

Romans 3:25

For the LORD is good; his mercy is everlasting; and his truth endureth to all generations.

HIS love endures forever

Psalm 100:5

We are bound to thank God always for
you, brethren, as it is meet, because
that your faith groweth exceedingly,
and the charity of every one of you all
toward each other aboundeth;

2 Thessalonians 1:3

The LORD is nigh unto them that are of a broken heart, and saveth such as be of a contrite spirit. Psalm 34:18

I have not hid thy righteousness
within my heart; I have declared
thy faithfulness and thy
salvation: I have not concealed
thy loving kindness and thy truth
from the great congregation.

Psalm 40:10

Love is the song sung by a grateful heart

Till we all come in the unity of
the faith, and of the knowledge
of the Son of God, unto a perfect
man, unto the measure of the
stature of the fulness of Christ:

Ephesians 4:13

I am an imperfect person loved by a perfect God.

But now is made manifest, and by the scriptures of the prophets, according to the commandment of the everlasting God, made known to all nations for the obedience of faith:

Romans 16:26

AND ABOVE ALL THESE THINGS PUT ON CHARITY,
WHICH IS THE BOND OF PERFECTNESS.   COL. 3:14

But my faithfulness and my mercy
shall be with him: and in my name
shall his horn be exalted.

Psalm 89:24

My heart rejoiceth in the Lord.

1 Samuel 2:1

And, behold, they brought to him a man sick of the palsy, lying on a bed: and Jesus seeing their faith said unto the sick of the palsy; Son, be of good cheer; thy sins be forgiven thee.

Matthew 9:2

And we have known and believed the love that God hath to us. God is love; and he that dwelleth in love dwelleth in God, and God in him.

1 John 4:16

Buried with him in baptism, wherein also
ye are risen with him through the faith
of the operation of God, who hath raised
him from the dead.

Colossians 2:12

Greater love hath no man than this, that a man lay down his life for his friends. John 15:13

Through faith we understand that the
worlds were framed by the word of God,
so that things which are seen were not
made of things which do appear.

Hebrews 11:3

For God hath not given us the spirit of fear; but of power, and of love, and of a sound mind.

2 Timothy 1:7

By faith Noah, being warned of God of things
not seen as yet, moved with fear, prepared an
ark to the saving of his house; by the which
he condemned the world, and became heir of
the righteousness which is by faith.

Hebrews 11:7

There is no fear in love; but perfect love casteth out fear: because fear hath torment. He that feareth is not made perfect in love.

1 John 4:18

Looking unto Jesus the author and finisher of our faith; who for the joy that was set before him endured the cross, despising the shame, and is set down at the right hand of the throne of God.

Hebrews 12:2

I will run the way of thy commandments, when thou shalt enlarge my heart. Psalm 119:32

Paul, a servant of God, and an apostle
of Jesus Christ, according to the faith
of God's elect, and the acknowledging
of the truth which is after godliness;

Titus 1:1

To the end he may stablish your hearts unblameable in holiness before God, even our Father, at the coming of our Lord Jesus Christ with all his saints.

1 Thessalonians 3:13

Here is the patience of the saints: here are they that keep the commandments of God, and the faith of Jesus.

Revelation 14:12

And the heavens shall praise thy
wonders, O Lord: thy faithfulness also
in the congregation of the saints.

Psalm 89:5

Love
believeth
all
things
1 Corinthians 13:7

O Lord, thou art my God; I will exalt
thee, I will praise thy name; for thou hast
done wonderful things; thy counsels of
old are faithfulness and truth.

Isaiah 25:1

Let the peace of God rule in your hearts.

Colossians 3:15

And Jesus said unto them, Because of your
unbelief: for verily I say unto you, If ye have
faith as a grain of mustard seed, ye shall say
unto this mountain, Remove hence to yonder
place; and it shall remove; and nothing shall
be impossible unto you.

Matthew 17:20

He brought me to the banqueting house and His banner over me was LOVE

Song of Solomon 2:4

So then they which be of faith are
blessed with faithful Abraham.

Galatians 3:9

And to know the love of Christ, which passeth knowledge, that ye might be filled with the fulness of God.

Ephesians 3:19

Seest thou how faith wrought
with his works, and by works
was faith made perfect?

James 2:22

LOVE HOPETH ALL THINGS

1 Corinthians 13:7

Not for that we have dominion over
your faith, but are helpers of your joy:
for by faith ye stand.

2 Corinthians 1:24

LOVE is KIND

Never fails · Always trusts · Is not proud · It seeking · Always hopes · Keeps no record of wrongs · Is not self

1 Corinthians 13:4-13

Yea, a man may say, Thou hast faith, and I have works: shew me thy faith without thy works, and I will shew thee my faith by my works.

James 2:18

Love endureth all things

1 Corinthians 13:7

For every one that asketh receiveth; and
he that seeketh findeth; and to him that
knocketh it shall be opened.

Matthew 7:8

My heart rejoiceth in the Lord

1 Samuel 2:1

Knowing this, that the trying of
your faith worketh patience.

James 1:3

Serve one another in love

Galatians 5:13

Know therefore that the Lord thy God, he
is God, the faithful God, which keepeth
covenant and mercy with them that love
him and keep his commandments to a
thousand generations;

Deuteronomy 7:9

I have found the one whom my soul loves

Song of Solomon 3:4

Hearken, my beloved brethren, Hath not
God chosen the poor of this world rich in
faith, and heirs of the kingdom which he
hath promised to them that love him?

James 2:5

If we love one another, God dwelleth in us, and His love is perfected in us. 1 John 4:12

So then faith cometh by hearing,
and hearing by the word of God.

Romans 10:17